Copyright @ 2008 by Audrey Michelle

The views, concepts, and opinions expressed in this book are solely those of the author and not intended to reflect or represent the opinions and or beliefs of any other person, persons or organizations.

Library of Congress Control Number: 2008930722

ISBN 978-09766787-5-6

Manufactured in the United States of America

An original publication by VonChasePublishing Company

VonChasePublishing Company
P.O Box 623
Winchester, CA 92596

All rights reserved

No part of this publication may be reproduced, stored in or introduced to a retrieval system, or transmitted, in any form, or by any means, (electronic, mechanical, photocopying, recording, or otherwise), without the prior written permission of both the copyright owner and the publisher of this book except by a reviewer who may quote brief passages in a review.

Formatting by Audrey Michelle

Vanity? The Pieces of Audrey Michelle

Kaleidoscope by Kylerado - Photography by Rolf Bertram

Parental Advisory

This publication includes some adult content

Table of Contents

Vanity?	10
Author's Biography	12
Dedication	14
Testimonials	15
Vanity? The Pieces of Audrey Michelle	23
Abuse Abuser	24
You Were Supposed to Love Me	25
Follow My Lead - Erotic	26
Fade to Light	28
Innocent	29
Heart Shaped Pills	30
A Life of Sleep	32
False Front	33
Within A Simple Stare	35
My Best Friend	36
I Can Handle You – Can You Handle Me? – Erotic	38
Bringing Sexy Back – Erotic	41
Flattened Story	42
Hardened Past	43
My Buried Seeds	44
Private Encore – Erotic	46
Disposable Girl	48
I Can't Baby	49
Analytical Flower	50
Forever Left Behind	52
It is Better to Have…	53
Blinded Need	54
MySpace Addict	56

Instigator – Erotic	58
Lapsed Fear	60
Lost Morals	62
Fated Scorn	63
Next in Row	64
Nice? – Erotic	65
My Own Worst Demons	67
Fingerprint in Time	68
Fear the Thunder	69
Growing Younger	70
Full-Filling – Erotic	72
Drowned Abyss	74
Lust Cannot Be 'Cause	75
I've Been	77
Didn't Mean to Hurt You	78
Hidden Truth	80
A New Woman – Erotic	83
'Cause	84
The Endless Stroll	86
Still Searching	88
Insatiable – Erotic	90
Mechanics of a Broken Heart	91
Before Ever and Forever	92
Generic	94
Pale Skin is Thicker	95
Partaking – Erotic	96
Big City Girl	97
Sail of Fate	98
Once Lovers - Now Strangers	100
Only in Deep Sleep Can This Be	102

Merry-Go-Round	103
Me and You and Our Rendezvous - Erotic	104
Season's Riddle	105
Torn Security	106
My Biggest Secret	108
Love in Lines	110
Restrained Dance	111
Playtime – Erotic	112
Stone Me	114
You Left Me Once	115
Why I've Been Late	116
To Obtain – Erotic	117
Vacant Hole	118
To the General Male Population – Part One	120
To the General Male Population – Part Two	122
Smile and No One Else Shall Know	124
Automatic Teller Machine – Erotic	126
The Life of a Flower	128
My Last Emotion	130
While Left Dying	132
Touch Unspoken	133
Your Man – Erotic	134
While Beauty Fades	136
Too Good to Be Forgotten	137
You	138
The Ticket – Erotic	140
It Couldn't Have Not Mattered	142
The Apple's Sound	143
Looking For Mr. Goodbar – Erotic	144
Incarcerated	146

S&M 148
The Survival of the Fittest 150
Combustible – Erotic 152
Desired Apple 154
Spoil Me Baby – Erotic 155
The Good Girl 157
Through the Window 158
Passive 160
While They Lay Sleeping 161
Attention Deficit Hyperactivity Disorder 163
Cupid's Broken Arrow 164
Sink or Swim 166
At Your Disposal – Erotic 167
Path Unhidden 168
A Naked Face 169
Credits 170

Vanity?

"You gain strength, courage and confidence by every experience in which you really stop to look fear in the face. You are able to say to yourself, 'I have lived through this horror. I can take the next thing that comes along.' You must do the thing you think you cannot do."

-- **Eleanor Roosevelt**

Standing bare for all to see
Feelings exposed, deep and passionate

Standing bare for all to see
Body exposed, confident and proud

Embarrassed of seeming too vain
Fearful more of going unnoticed
Is there vanity within the image reflected?

A capsule of pain
Little balls of lies and hurt rotate through me
Bump against each other just for laughs

A falling star
Destined to glow passionately
Yet to fall alone through the sky

A warrior
Willingly losing the will to fight
Enemies growing, now too many to defeat

A baby girl
Carried within the body of a woman
Can hear her cry, yet can't reach her

A princess
Constantly awaiting her prince to come
Assuming contentedness in kissing frogs

An aging starlight
Always the center of attention
Knowing she is too old for her life

A woman
Doing the one thing she thought she could not do
Praying that Eleanor Roosevelt was right

Author's Biography

Billy the Kid Studios

Audrey Michelle was born the middle of three daughters to a close-knit family in Baltimore, Maryland. She started writing poetry at a young age and submitted her poems to national contests. One early poem about a Snowman that retains his wooden smile even after melting away demonstrated an early interest and understanding in both the fragility of life and the resilience of the human spirit. This interest is evident still in the poems she writes today.

As an adolescent and college student, Audrey drifted from her interest in writing, but life events inspired her to once again commit her emotions to paper. Immediately following her graduation from the University of Maryland at College Park, Audrey moved to San Diego, California. She worked in different sales-related professions and opened a speed-dating service before getting married and becoming a Stay-at-Home-Mom to her son, Gavin, while pursuing a dual Masters Degree. She soon resumed her entrepreneurial work in the establishment of an Internet children's clothing store and a web design service while still in San Diego. Audrey

and her family moved to Tampa Bay, Florida and quickly thereafter she found she was pregnant a second time. Tragically, when Audrey was 6 ½ months pregnant the child, Chase Victoria, was lost, bringing about a flood of difficult and painful emotions. Soon thereafter she and her husband divorced.

Despite an extremely difficult few years, Audrey is determined to maintain a sense of self and resolve in life. Battling depression, but keeping hopeful in the path that life will take her, Audrey once again uses her writing to work out her most difficult and complex of emotions. She has found an online community of friends and fans who continue to provide nurture and support through the invaluable commentary and conversation that her writing inspires. Hoping that her poems will provide comfort and inspiration for those who read it, she writes of her deepest emotions. Still living in the Tampa Bay area with her greatest support and accomplishment, Gavin.

Audrey is proud to present her first published collection of writing.

****

For more information on Audrey Michelle please visit her profile at:

www.myspace.com/audreyliles

Dedication

This Book Is Dedicated To:

Friendship found within a life of solitude
Ears of love that listened to an ailing mind
Realness in a life of tin
The acceptance of a desperate, lonely soul
Those around the world that believed in a broken shell

My readers and supporters
You are the friends I've never known
You are my strength

Thank you for saving me from my own worst enemy

This book is also dedicated to my son Gavin Jacob Liles who offers me the truest of all my smiles

Testimonials

How many gaze with unobservant eyes
To cheer their mind and watch her flesh is their delight
Her secret thoughts remain concealed
Yes, she is beauty beyond compare
But they never see the wise, the musing, meditative mind
They lust after a glittering constellation in the starry skies
To me my angel's high intelligence has been revealed
The beauty on the inside is all I see
High thoughts and feelings make me wonder
Seeing they see only sublime visions
No words of my wisdom will they understand
They will only think she looks so divine
Francis Fury - Akron, OH

I thank Audrey Michelle for being a great friend who I deeply respect. For having a heart when all seems not right. She's had the words that crossed my path. She gave the words to me during the year that lifted my heart. She gave to me a reason to go on when all seems so wrong at times.
Ray Hanger - Chicago, IL

Audrey Michelle is beautiful and bold, but most of all she is a real person, a mother and talented writer who has loved and lost, still standing independently tall and using those experiences to share the captivating and sometimes vulnerable complexities of woman. Audrey's sexy and moving attitude pours through her words, perfectly blending desire and understanding...
Stacy A. Foster (Virtual Flower) - Indiana

It is obvious from reading Audrey Michelle's poetry that she has suffered great pain and loss. One would think simply by looking at her physical beauty that she is doing wonderfully. Not so. However, what she has done is take that pain and put it on paper. Her rising strength is evident in her work. She has put it in such a way that many can relate to her experiences in their own way. Being able to relate to a poet's words is the signature of a good poet. Here, you have one.
Art Noble - Jensen Beach, FL
Poet and Author, "The Sacred Female"

There are so many things that come to mind when I think of Audrey. It would be more than obvious to write or talk about her body and extreme good looks. But that's just the surface and really doesn't do justice to the woman she really is. There is a level of complexity to her sensitivity not only with herself but to others as well. Her artistic musings coupled by her intoxicated voice guide you through realms of passion and desire at the same time allow you to see through her own personal rose colored glasses. Audrey is a sheer joy to know and one of my favorite mysteries.

Sean C Brown (Clandestine Rumor) - Boca Raton, FL

Audrey Michelle is absolutely the hottest girl I know. I am amazed by her body, mind, face, talent, and heart.

Tonya Scott - Los Angeles, CA - Singer

Audrey's worth far surpasses anything a camera can catch. The richness of her eyes shows my spirit many things....Anyone that has had the chance to talk to her on the phone or hear her over the internet knows she is so much more than a pretty face and sexy body. She is phenomenal and I adore her!!

Marcella Beaulieu (Poetic Pink) - California

Where do I begin in describing the ink of Audrey Michelle? Who can be sensual and poignant, salient and clever, inspirational and surreal. You can feel her joy and desperation with every breath; you reminisce and contemplate in every thought. Her words are confronting in their honesty because the lady is so real.

Crashimp - Sydney, New South Wales, Australia

Miss Audrey, Miss Audrey, I am shaking my head, reading your stuff is like taking a breath after being underwater too long. You just made my top ten, I must say, I am a hard critic when it comes to poetry and writing. I don't expect any less from people that know how to write because they are capable of excellence if they apply themselves and not do a half ass job. I don't usually give compliments. You have real talent and so much honesty, it's not fake, no showing off, very literal and so relieving. Your stuff is modern and it shows where poetry is going, this is what dreams are made of:

> "We were going to plant that tree
> Someday in the backyard

Of the house we would share
No idea where
That was just Geography though

Our kids were going to climb it
They would have had your dark skin
With my green eyes
We planned them too
I really envisioned our children
That too wasn't a lie"
(excerpt from Didn't Mean to Hurt You)

Sylvia Plath just turned in her grave
Graceland - Poet

There are attractive women who open a man's eyes and awaken his loins. Then there are beautiful women who open a man's soul and awaken the greatness of his own spirit. There's a sense of power about you, more than even Helen of Troy.

I think you might be here to kick ass in the world, uplifting versus destroying.

Inner Strength - Orlando, FL

I have only know Audrey a short while, but have grown to love her as a true friend and poet. Her words, whether written or spoken, speak miles to my heart. Her imagery and unique use of styles keeps you at the edge of each write. I feel that I have gained a great knowledge of who Audrey Michelle is and wants to be: A phenomenal person and Author.
Lori Ann Vieth (Poetic Mama Bear) - Alabama

Audrey Michelle's writing is raw and bare; it's how we all feel, no sugarcoating. Her words offer the gift of expression one can feel. There are no boundaries in her creativity and she proves that in each word she writes. Every word has meaning... Limits are made to be defied and she does that well!
Healium Shriekspear - Bremerton, Washington

I thought Audrey was an exhibitionist kind of female. Writers who frequent MySpace and look for drooling pseudo critics, until I read her amazing poetry! She exhibits depth in her work which I find very unique in thought content and she is able to project an aspect about which one has not even thought to look for! Her areas of creativity extend well beyond her poems as can be seen from her varied style of work and her profound way of probing into the depths of the human mind! She is a lovely human being first, a great friend and a very warm person at heart!

Cautious - India

I have known Audrey through her marvelous writings for over a year and a half now. I find her to be an extremely intelligent person, who can convey her thoughts very succinctly and clearly. The beauty of her writing lies in the brevity of her suggestive poems which are encapsulated and composed to convey the complete feelings in a very few well structured words.

The subtle underlying erotic content is sufficient to excite the feeblest of minds, she is a master of weaving tantalizing words in to a carpet of sexuality which stuns the reader and turns them into drooling subjects! Much like her pictures which are exotic, beautiful and yet not vulgar and leave the viewer gasping for more!

Each of her writings conveys whatever deep thought has inspired her to put down on paper. She carefully considers her words and thoughts so that they fit her readers, she carries out this task admirably and being techno-savvy she keeps up with the tools available on the net to make her reading more gripping for the readers.

She is an amazing multi talented personality and I am sure there is much more to her then what we see on the net, she combines tremendous visuals of her amazing body with a razor sharp mind, a true beauty and mind combination which is so pleasant to know personally.

She is a tremendous friend who does not hesitate to offer advice when requested and goes out of the way to help people; she in fact has a huge golden heart in that envious body and excellent mind!

In simple words I wait for her erotic poetry blogs diligently and try to grasp (keep gasping) the meaning as much as I can and am indeed honored to have her as a friend on MySpace and pray to the almighty to give a chance to acquaint her in real life as well. I wish her all the success and fame; she truly deserves every bit of it!!
Rasputin - Singapore

Soft sultry tones are possessed in her voice. She captures emotions in words that sing to my own heart. Often her poetry expresses so many sides of the emotions, erotic, passionate, yearning, and loving all rolled together so perfectly. Men love her for her beauty both mentally and physically, women love her for expressing the emotions we so often wish we could express so beautifully while we also admire her intelligence and beauty. I highly recommend all read my dear friends words.
Mary Hazen Fultondale (Mary Ska) - Alabama

How does one who writes agony,
With the stroke of ecstasy,
Give pain while revealing joy,
Audrey is an enigma,
Of fantasy truth in reality,
She reveals the pain in all of us,
Only to let us know we are not alone,
What a friend I have found in her.
Wizthom (wisemanspeeks) - Akron, Ohio

I was thrilled to meet Audrey in person one Thanksgiving in Baltimore, after reading her poetry and participating in her erotic writing contests on MySpace. She is every bit as charming, witty, talented, and intelligent in real life as she is within her writing.
Mike Hmielewski (Mr. Ex) - Maryland

Audrey Michelle has acquired an extensive following of dedicated readers and fellow authors whose remarks extol the virtues of her literary talents.

The author's acclaimed original works are evocative, sensual, compelling, moving and struck with vivid imagery to satisfy all of one's senses. Her words examine the human relationship with stark clarity, maturity, depth and are so very rich in texture, color, sensitivity and self-awareness.

This writer embraces in her works directness and purity that begs close examination.

Audrey Michelle is a wonderfully gifted author worthy of the praise her contemporary yet timeless word craft have generated. Her publications are indeed a must-read.

Don MacIver - Victoria, British Columbia, Canada
Author, "Journeys in Verse"

From the moment I read her first poem, I have been truly captivated and enchanted. Audrey Michelle writes with such sweet eloquence and conviction, it's hard not to take a breath and sigh after every line. Her poetry is real and genuine for it is scribed from her own heart's experiences. Audrey Michelle's poems will touch your heart, heighten your senses, embrace your mind and enlighten your soul indefinitely!

Jayne Sevrin - New York

Audrey Michelle writes with the passion Gloria Estefan sings. Following what seemed to be career ending tragedy, Gloria Estefan emerged to perform like never before her work, "Coming out of the Dark."

Every line of Audrey Michelle's work is like emerging from the darkness of illiteracy and ignorance to the light of seeing clearly our way to live and love. Her words move from ecstatic pain to ecstatic bliss in a breath until you sigh like excellent love has just been made that will give birth to new hope and new vision.

Feel her passion. Breathe her spirit. Feel the sensual and the sacred power dance in words. Feel Audrey Michelle's voice.

Oscar Lee Crawford - Arizona
http://oscarcrawford.blogspot.com

From the moment I first started a poetry MySpace Page, I was an instant fan of Audrey Michelle and when I first read "Fantasy" on April 5th of 2006, I was in love. From the very beginning Audrey was taking poetry to the next level in the form of Erotic Poetry. A brilliant style of eroticism of the spoken word and on October 15th of 2006, Audrey first hit MySpace with "Innocent?" an erotic spoken word poem! When I heard that piece, I knew Audrey was indeed an artist! Audrey Michelle has been a mentor to many aspiring writers young and old, myself included. In her humility, she found herself, an inner voice which transformed her life experiences to help her readers in all aspects of their lives. This ability has become her

passion to which she displays in an array of talents that she passes on to her peers. She is confident, compassionate, and witty! Audrey has taken me on a jubilant ride full of passion, and I am honored that she is my friend. Audrey Michelle, thank you for all your guidance, understanding and patience that you have given to all of us.

Robert "Chief" Garza - Oklahoma

On my journey into learning more about myself in spirit, heart and soul, I was touched and inspired by Audrey Michelle's poetic words of depth and soulful meaning. Audrey writes true from the heart and soul. A gifted writer that exposes what one could only take away from reading a sense of, "you've lived it".

Every word of every verse grabbed my spirit's strength to pursue my own visions and dreams.

Laurie Warth - Missouri

Audrey is not only beauty on the outside but she is beauty on the inside, one of the most amazing poets of our times....her poetry is sensitive and sensual....... a joy to the readers senses.......her poetry is beauty

Moses Roth - Israel

There are so many words that many have used to try to describe Audrey Michelle, to equate her, to capture her; but I have found that no one word can simply translate the imprint her essence leaves on the canvas of one's heart. To say she leads one to embark upon creativity; is to only gather a glimpse into her hearts mind.

To call her eloquent; is to try to sum up a sunset's brilliance and paint it with the limitations of the brush prints of a word. To admire her strength; is to think you have uncovered the mystery of Stonehenge.

The REDDEST OF ROSES:
She truly is, fire and brilliance, fragile yet enduring, all that the petals of life could ever mend together to form, is found in the mist of her budding smile. It has truly been an honor and a privilege to call her my friend and to share a place in her life... I love you my RED...
                                                Mykell (REFLECTIONS) - Hawaii

Audrey Michelle writes with depth, intelligence and from the heart. She is fascinating, sexy and she sure can write.
                                                Roger Lindstrom (Easy Rog) - Massachusetts

Audrey's physical allure is like a fine lace veil, once it is removed an inner light is revealed, reflected in her writings. Audrey's poetry is not always pretty: it's sometimes raw, yet always real...These truths are written from her heart, reflect her soul, and often wink confidently at life as if to say, "Yeah, I gotcha!" I joyfully bask in her light!
                                                Dauphine E Sowell {Ferocious Kitten} - Georgia

Vanity?

The Pieces of Audrey Michelle

Abuse Abuser

Once upon a time I felt the beauty of an entangled existence
As another body coated my soul
With the sweat of true acceptance

It soaked it into my needy pores
Disease infected through its absorption
Constantly intoxicated by new found spirituality
You were my prince

And I **WAS** your princess

The angel that saved you from a life of falsity
Where there had been dark
G-d said
"Let there be light"

Your skin pressed against mine in a seemingly everlasting embrace

The drops of adoration I so desperately desired
Slowly become diluted
Mixed with chemicals of sedation
That put my mind into a comatose state of surrender
Digesting each piece of my reality
Replacing it with the guilt, fear and depression of addiction

Surviving for the rare samples of my short lived highs
From which withdrawal always ensued
At times seemingly fatal

Still I felt the strength of legs entangle
The grip of your need to demean me
To suffocate my G-D given right to the pursuit of happiness

Yet, I required my fix
I found myself at rock bottom
Licking anything that even resembled a glimpse of awe
Off a floor filthy with belittlement

Recovering now
My limbs roam naked
Always they shall yearn
For the drops of Jupiter they once tasted

You Were Supposed To Love Me

You were supposed to love me
When the moon got too dim to light the night sky

I live within the box of that promise
Somehow float within the flimsy exterior your intentions created
Hurt in the memory of a dream that never existed

The sun descends and my heart grows black with the sky
Pumps to the beat of an empty space
Where
Anatomically
Yours was supposed to exist

Were you ever really there when the night grew dark?

My hand felt your skin
As your fingers tightened around its fragile stems
Strangled them so tightly
That the mystery could no longer breathe

Your arms did hold me
Like vines they entangled me
Surrounded me with their needs
Pleaded with me to never leave

My legs wrapped around your hips
And I swear I felt you enter my soul

You weren't supposed to leave me
Within the memory of a promise
That floats upon a pitch black dream

Follow My Lead – Erotic

Want to get dirty with me?
Come here, follow my lead

My prey
My feed
Let me take you
Utterly make you understand
What it truly means
To be a man
Want to get me hot
Hit my spot
Assure yourself
A whole in one shot
I need to seduce
Male multi orgasm proof
Hot ass body at use
Top stripper dance moves
Clothing removed
So damn hard
That I know he approves
Imagine the views
My ass in a groove
Winding
Grinding
Mute, deaf and blinding
Utopia finding
Body heightened
Mind enlightened
Future now brightened
Kegeled hole tightened
Testosterone in rage
Peak reaching stage
Orgasm my wage
The pay for my act
My body reacts
Epileptic attack
Vibrating rack

Screaming
No holding back
Self esteem unrestricted
The best un-contradicted
Porno star depicted
Deepest of pleasure inflicted

Surgeon General warns
My sex is addictive

Fade to Light

Fear assumes all hope as false
Declares a war to prove its loss
The sin within a mind that's proud
Ignored first pinpricks it allowed
Doubts chubby fingers steal belief
Leaves behind prints of its grief
Within its smudge its armies grow
Will powers rule they over throw
Hopes soldiers fight through acid rain
To find all of its troops remained
A flashlight found on injured shred
Lights up a black path found ahead
Fate orders units to proceed
"Follow dark, to light it leads"
Rain slows down but still drips fear
Drops fought each time they come near
Clouds silver lining then appears
To dry the land of useless tears
A vision left behind rains shower
Shines hues along the path to power
Though hope spends all it must invest
In arch that leads to treasure chest

Innocent?

She sleeps within Bordeaux satin sheets

Bathes in the finest imported French bath salts

Meticulously dresses in the hottest designer apparel

Applies her make-up as carefully as an artist
    Finishing the last strokes of a masterpiece

Yet leaves the house feeling dirty

The guilt inside consumes her

And nothing covers the ugliness of shame

Heart Shaped Pills

Do you whisper sweet "nothings" in her ear too?
Or was that sweet talk reserved just for me?

"Our bubble" we used to call it
I spoke to you as you slept
"My Knight in shining armor"
Lancelot, capturing me from a world of fire breathing dragons

Our first kiss consumed me with truth
Knowledge it was to be my last first kiss

A feeling so pure couldn't mislead

Pills slipped to me daily
Cruelty released in milligrams
Dosage increased as dependency grew

Pills were heart shaped, inscribed with comments

"What's wrong with you"?
"Tell mommy she's nuts"
"What are you stupid"?
"I married you to make you a better person"
"No one else will want you, you're used property"

Immunity to your drug grew
Dosage increased, caused overdose

The heat of dragons again consumes
Within a castle built on hope

Do you feed her the same pills?
Sugar to lure in the bait
An ever increasing after taste of bitterness

Perhaps she's the princess you were meant to rescue
The conversation hearts offered me etched with only the truth

Julio Cesar Custom Photography

A Life Of Sleep

Once fell asleep within the arms
Of empty words and hollow charm
A fate that seemed the will of G-D
In time, learned will to be façade
Love was assumed and heart was deceived
Slumber prescribed and pain was relieved

Continuous, nights dream was known
Believed until days light was shown
Rays blindfolded view of sleeps hope
For peace in mind once mind awoke
Day after night a war was fought
Views innate vs. views been taught

Doubts wished to force instincts surrender
Seemed strong against weakened contender
Armies were found in depths of thought
To fight for need that dreams begot
Fear fought a hard and noble fight
Though wakened eyes now offered sight

Hope pried them from their endless sleep
Once free, fate took its self named leap

Forever seems the fall in length
Tested each day is inner strength
Doubts still threaten morbid attack
Fear still beckons the mind to turn back
Since endless seems the fall from leap
Eyes sometimes ache for life of sleep

False Front

A perfect lie
I can't deny
The pain inside
Emotional ride
Twisting, turning
Overall mourning
Screeching, crawling
Vaulting aside
Movement covers
The pain inside
Extremely low
More then I show
If you could know
The pain inside
A smile to hide
Grace I provide
Friends at my side
All just to lie
Just to cover
From any other
The empty lonely
Pain inside

Within A Simple Stare

There's heat within a simple stare
A burn within a hungry glare

Devoured by a pair of eyes
Above a sound, intensified
Fingertips across the chords
Sounds vibrate along a board

There's heat within a simple stare
It views and lights a bodies flare

Electrified by latent heat
A throb that fills a hole complete
Although two bodies never meet
The two can share an aching beat

There's heat within a simple stare
Through audio its pleasure blares

A voice that flames a peak inside
Each time with ears it coincides
Touch that's delivered just by sight
Can cause ones insides to ignite

There's heat within a simple stare
Its passion forced through waves of air

Copyright 2007 by Audrey Michelle
http://www.myspace.com/audreyliles

Graphic by Zelle

Within A Simple Stare

There's heat within a simple stare
      A burn within a hungry glare

Devoured by a pair of eyes
Above a sound, intensified
Fingertips across the chords
Sounds vibrate along a board

There's heat within a simple stare
        It views and lights a bodies flare

Electrified by latent heat
A throb that fills a hole complete
Although two bodies never meet
The two can share an aching beat

There's heat within a simple stare
        Through audio its pleasure blares

A voice that flames a peek inside
Each time with ears it coincides
Touch that's delivered just by sight
Can cause ones insides to ignite

There's heat within a simple stare
        Its passion forced through waves of air

My Best Friend

I remember your smile

It lit up any broken heart I picked up
While walking down the path of friendship

We walked together
Loved music
Pure laughter
Genuine tears
Raw honesty
Secret crimes

My best friend

I was so proud
When people said we looked like sisters

You were my idol
I wonder if I ever told you

The thought that I might look like you
A goddess on earth
But real
Real like I'd never imagined

You brought me up
When others tore me down
Made me feel like I could accomplish anything

I was soaring
And you the wind
That blew me higher

With you
I knew my truths
I had no choice
I couldn't lie to you

And you always asked
You always cared

But you changed
You hurt me
Neglected
Emptied
Destroyed

My hero didn't
Need me
        Love me
                Bring me up
Even notice me anymore

We tried to maintain a friendship
Things never were the same

The realness was gone
We both knew it

You disappeared emotionally
Then physically

Is it your spell or my need for acceptance?

After all
        The pain
                Neglect
                        Heartbreak
                              Fear
                                      Insecurity
You brought into my life

I miss you

Still

I Can Handle You - Erotic

I can handle you
Can you handle me?

For you I'll manage
To cause real damage
To my reputation
Across the nation
You
The instigation
For syndication
They'll call me a freak
With sex technique
But I'll be your whore
Keep you wanting more
In bed I roar
Your spirit will soar
My legs will lure
They'll be the bait
Won't make you wait
Let's consummate
Deliver a beating
Keep you screaming
Your muscles will ache
Won't have to fake
Know that you're good
That's understood
The best in town
But I'm better
A record setter
Can't get any wetter
You'll need more
See what's in store
Have me on the floor
Won't lock the door
So what if they see
They'll just wish to be
Either you or me

Everywhere
In every room
On every table
In the shower
Feel water's power
Take in your full tower
I won't gag
A talent I have to share with you
Imagine that view
All the way down
Make sure to advise
Want to master the technique
Make all of you weak
Ensure that you leak
Before you peak
If it's orgasm you seek
Make me your sheik

**Do you desire
To be acquired?**

Billy the Kid Studios

Bringing Sexy Back - Erotic

Bringing sexy back
Mastering the tact
Making the good last
Expect a deep impact
Spasms through your legs
Eyes rolled back
Toes in fist
Mind a bliss
Isn't just a tryst
Every day
Every night
Holding your sword
So very tight
Can't get enough
Got to have the goods
Keep my hands tied
Blindfold my eyes
Master my thighs
Awaiting your rise
Stroke the lady
Make her squirm
All the spasms
I now earned
Thank you for
The return
That's the way
It's gotta be
Down on you
Then down on me
Search for treasure
You will find
More than imagined
Amplified

Flattened Story

Falling for an unknown past
Handfuls of still photographs
Shot long ago, camera naïve
Its view of love, never received
Exposures stored throughout the years
Of lovers known that disappeared
Moments snapped became embedded
Pictures etched were then regretted

Stored moments, "Once upon a times"
Of fairytales and nursery rhymes
"Lonely ever after", stories ended
Novels survived, though not as intended
Once kissed each prince became a frog
All toads that jumped love log to log
Leaped from a heart misunderstood

Princess was viewed as only wood
Photos faded, books are closed
Film of love has been exposed
Forever lives within dark rooms
Knights are frogs within costumes
True queens don't find their destined kings
Flash flicks and kings become just flings
A foggy lens now blurs the script
Love is 2D and fate was gypped

Hardened Past

The moment fleets and then it's gone
While the chance passed, you sat withdrawn

I hammered but produced no hole
In the cement around your soul
I begged to enter, but wasn't selected
There is no entrance to a heart protected

Walls I punched with arms of care
Their concrete poured by late despair
Sheets left behind by those who've lied
Are fossilized within white pride

The words directed to your ears
Cannot be heard through what adheres
From powder sprinkled in the past
Now hardened pain
                And it shall last…

This moment must fleet, with its pain
For fear of coating I'd retain

My Buried Seeds

The seeds of love
I continuously bury
Began to sprout in the spring

Feelings blossomed slowly
Survived the summer's heat

Autumns breezes blew the petals
Off the stems of my soul

Raised my body off the ground
Heaven bound

The winds strengthened
Tornados of emotions encircled me

Forced
My heart rotated fast
And I became a prisoner
To the passion I desired so deeply

Winter was too cold
Cloud nine froze

The ice brittle
I fell through

Dropped fast
Crashed to the ground

My heart released
From the winds of love
That made me soar so high

Again I bury my seeds
Water them
Feed them
Nurture them

Hoping this season's flower
Will be brighter then the last

Hoping that perhaps
This year

I'll forever skate on ice

Private Encore - Erotic

Look at the curves; watch them unfold
Feet pressed against the silver pole
They descend as I twist around
Quickened pace, not slowing down

Movements learned and then perfected
Performed against the rod erected

Next phase is under way
My body parts are on display
Clothing ripped and torn to shreds
As towards obsession you are led

Lights go out and all else leave
The bar staff has been relieved
Still I dance, unaware
Because I feel your presence there

Laid down flat at edge of stage
For this dance you must engage
Hips stir in subtle rhyme
Slowly, softly - dance rewinds

Now it's your pole
      I must climb

Enter me, but just a bit
Let me work just on the tip
Entice the hunger, then proceed
When want to enter becomes need

Your hips find my subtle groove
In time with mine their forced to move
One delivers, one receives
Feeding off each other's weave

Hand tugging on my chest
Fingers dance upon my crest
Transcended within the heat
My hips stop their aching beat

I thrust them high, your treat to seek
Till unified we reach our peak

You hold me tight and whisper "night"
Tomorrow offers new delights
A mystery in who I'll meet
As we role play within the sheets

Jon Burdick Photography

Disposable Girl

In retrospect,
life is a series of empty relationships
Too many have disappeared

My trashcan full of memories
I can't seem to take to the dump

The laughter
      Smiles
           Drama
                Pain
Balled up in a forever growing mass

In my dreams these people haunt me
I relive the times that to me were beautiful and meaningful
Awake to the realization
That I am the only one that holds on to them

Their lives continue on without me
I don't reside in their minds
Or in their trashcans

I've been burned with their worn out clothing years ago
Scorched for sins I don't understand
As few have cared enough to explain them

In my life I've missed many a goal
Yet somehow obtained some that I never desired to be
I am unnecessary, unneeded and unloved
By many I've held dear

There is nothing emptier then a full trashcan

I Can't Baby

Felt a fetus kick
Body altered over months
Adapted pregnant state

Loved her since a set of pink lines
Appeared on a magic mystery wand

Maternity clothing draped sadly in the closet
Ache to be worn for the full third trimester

In dreams, she cries to me

"Hold me mommy"

"I can't baby"

Her eyes green
      Like mine

Always full of tears
      Like mine

A vacancy left behind
Drowned in hollowness

There were no cries
Eyes seen only in sleep

"I can't baby"

Sometimes, I still feel her kick

Analytical Flower

Whirling, swirling
The flower dances like no other
Its petals plump with knowledge
Its confident hues seduce
With an aroma of pure passion

Their pollen leading their route
Bees flock to her
They find her movements intoxicating
And they seek to possess her

Once satisfied by her stamen
The bees move on
Her strong and independent stigma
Then seems intimidating

Other flowers stand close by
They know their role
And they portray it

Stance of beauty
Stillness of mind
Swaying only as expected winds blow

In speed with her neighbors
She now moves to a mute beat

Finding the stifle of true rejection
More restraining then a life of falseness

Forever Left Behind

Lips have remained wet
Since stained by your deceiving kiss
The taste of your cold breath
Still mingles with the shame inside my mouth

Handprints still bruise me
Grip me like an instrument
A drum pounded to the beat of an animal
Devouring its hollow prey

I bleed the ink of your name
Carelessly carved by your raging pen
That forever etched your signature
Into the enflamed depths of my very meaning

Remnants of your wrath
Cling to my disgraced skin
Coat a body still absorbed
With the belittlement you left behind

Jaroslaw Photography

It Is Better To Have...

I remember how you stared at me as I drove off
Your eyes sparkled, light beams of admiration

You used to speak to me in your sleep
Truth from the depths of your very soul
"You're my everything"

Felt as if I'd been clicked-into-place
Every time our eyes met across a crowded room
Final realization of happily ever after

Even through the hate you still loved me...

Disappointment poured from you like sweat
I slept in puddles of it, ate and drank it

Absorbed it into my own fluids and assumed it
A tortured soul, I plead with the night
Contently, you slept next to me
Nothing could fracture your rigidity
I tried all brands of words that slice

I hate you for the gift of love you gave me

    Perhaps without the loss of it,

        I could have slept contently too

Blinded Need

Turn her and face just her back
Close the eyes and see just black
    Shield her glow
        Then fear denies
That beauty shined within her eyes

Once layered, pupils can dismiss
The need they found within her kiss

Though hurt again by blocked off sight
The pain she feels won't end her fight
    Her eyes may blink
        But still shall see
'Cause only sight finds destiny

Though broken lies her mortal soul
And each rejection takes its toll

She holds the strength of fifty men
Within her thin and fragile stem
    Her blossoms droop
        But not for long
For she's a woman and she's strong

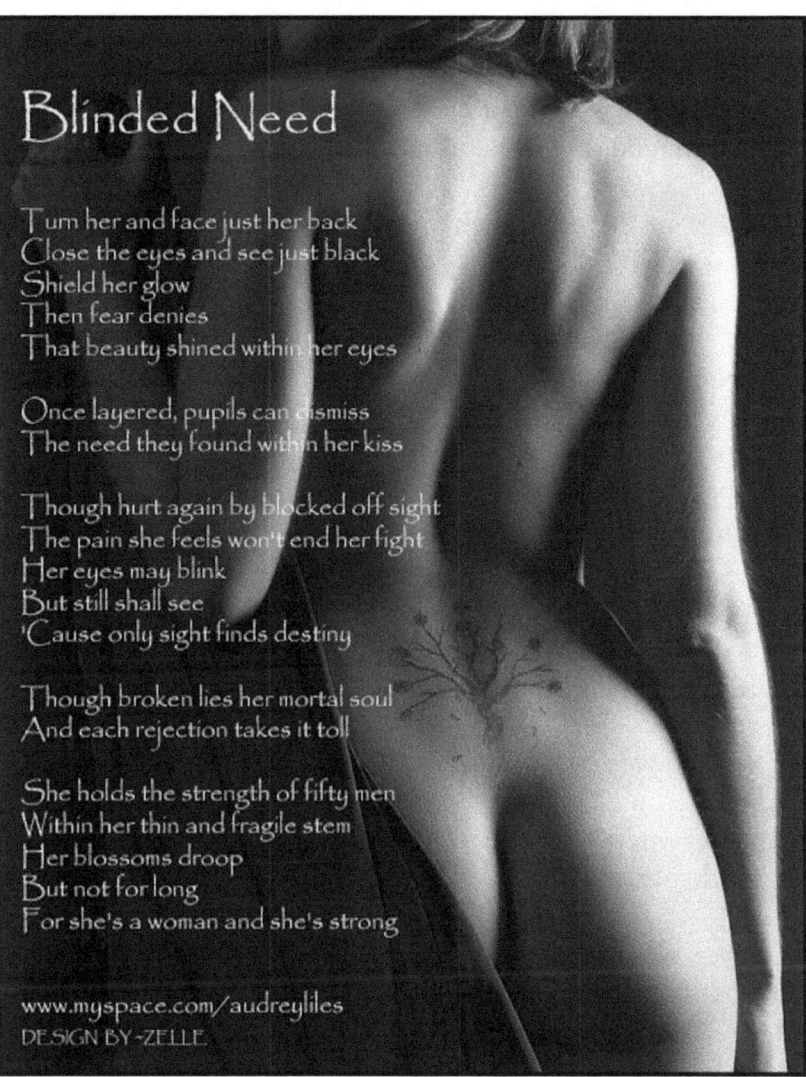

Graphic by Zelle

MySpace Addict

Night falls hard for the gold of heart
I want to run but I'm afraid to start

The doors are locked in each direction
I don't search for the key
As I've learned my lesson

The open doors cause disarray
So I stay inside
Afraid to play

Constant question

When's my day?

To feel the sun tan happy rays

My skin's so pale
And needs some light
No matter where
It's not that bright

I'm never seen for who I am
But what I seem to be to them

Others can't imagine
That I'm truly good
Though I write and I talk
I'm still not understood

So from my life I want to hide
Lock the door and live inside

I'll just exist
To you confide

Press post
Await your reply

I hope one day the pain subsides
And I can live a normal life

I still will make time to write to you
But maybe then with a new view

My online friends
You are my all
Without your thoughts

There's only walls

Instigator – Erotic

Just a giver
A head deliverer
Deep throat swallower
Intake monitor
Semi-Sonic
Deeply erotic

Grabbing on that stick
Suck
Ball lick, ball lick

Pressing firmly
On his boys
While I treat their daddy
Like a toy

Bounce him in and
Bounce him out
Amazingly
He's well-endowed

Love to pleasure it
Go down on it
Spit on it
Flick the tip of it
With my tongue
Reaching the tip down to my lungs

Reacting to his hips
They tell me how
To move my lips
How far to dip
Can't miss one drip

Need to swallow my feed
As he spits out his seed

****

I'm what gets his candle lit

His thoughts can't handle it
I'm good
It's not a myth
But he's the only one that knows it

Because I'm
His mistress
His angel
Horny manipulator

Always on his mind

Each night he gets
To enter inside
Slip and slide
Enjoy the ride
As our bodies collide

His women of dreams
Now his nightly regime

The highest peak
That one could seek

A lady in the street

But a freak in discreet

Lapsed Fear

A truth one must be blind to miss
Evaporates within each kiss

Deafness to a bell so loud
Justice plays without a sound

Girl desired if less real
To consume would mean to feel

Arid seems the land today
Rain shall not be chased away

Sin dissolves on false belief
What is offered, worth the keep

Lonely in a world too cruel
Honesty against the rules

Play the role; figure it out
Escape all one is about

Fight a fear that burns so strong
Fire lapses, not for long

Stare at her, with eyes content
Created image with intent

It lingers in a mind too dumb
To realize all she is, is numb

Rejection turned off all senses
Lives life now in iron fences

Remain within a dream not own
Princess captured; just on loan

Turn her in for one less red
Backs turn now on false instead

Lost Morals

Morals gained and morals lost
Spent in cents to pay pain's cost
A nickel here, a quarter there
Another charge on one once fair
Limitless, the limit seems
That value falls each time deceived
Once worth her weight within pure gold
Though cheapened each time bought and sold
Fortune offered, and then misused
Payment faltered, credit abused
Balance owed is too high to pay
To ever gain the worth that strayed
In fight to save a bankrupt heart
She lessened values she'd been taught
A beauty born was lost in trade
Each time she sold her soul away
The forecast proves an endless crash
Her debt too high to buy soul back
So here she sits, without value
Now nothing, but a girl "to do"

Fated Scorn

Cross a street to find ones home
A house in which they live alone
The windows shake and walls fall down
Rains impede with clapping sound
Ignore the noises, they're just fear
Close your eyes and they disappear

Sleep again through a nightmare
Or a dream that's worse by compare
Each offers hope that is obscene
Another wish to remain unseen
Forever's just a word that's spoken
Gone each time that one's awoken

Walk again in streets of fear
Scream to those who cannot hear
Realness, only covered tin
14 Karat dipped in sin
Flavored by a taste desired
Filled with only truth expired

A baby cries but can't yet see
The reasons why their tears shall flee
Each falls upon a ground too soaked
By tears decades before evoked
Another life of endless scorn
Occurs each time a child is born

Next In Row

Innocence proved only show
Signs all read, devoured slow

Blindness faked in vivid world
Transparent mask upon girl

Lessons taught through history
Feed a mind; no mystery

Smiling they stand in a row
Quicker falls each domino

Dots differ, number equal
Movie seen, view now sequel

Requiring a kind of deep
Company chosen just can't keep

Passion needy, no supply
Beg for feeding, be denied

Lustful, must be an illusion
Fear assuming such conclusion

In war of pride; will not fight
Falseness seeming out of sight

Forgive yet never forget
Take until point no regret

Smile and curtsy, no more show
Fully discovered, "next in row"

Nice? - Erotic

Nasty as I want to be
Don't you leave here
Stay with me

We'll play doctor
Hold me down
Kiss me softly
Fuck that... hard

Drive me crazy
With your ways see
Make me spacey
Teach me how baby

What will work
What will it take
To get you off
To make you shake

I promise skills that are off the chain
Just make me want to cum again

Charles Williams Photography

My Own Worst Demons

Ghosts illuminate like fire on a candle's wick
Each possesses their own name
    And personality by now

Reminders of the pain lived through
Each becoming more opaque with time passed

And I'm more scared now

I am so used to them
They've lingered in my life longer than any of flesh
Entertaining with words that constantly inspire pain

And they're here again

I feel their hands upon me
As they grip the confident shell
I've encased myself in
They peel it off piece by piece
Find a naked piece of skin
And inject into it more of their serum

The juice to which I'm now addicted
As if I require the shots

I allow them in
Open myself to their thoughts
A mental suicide

But the ghosts can't disappear
They are the only ones that have stayed

Fingerprint in Time

The imprint of your memory resides here
A fingerprint in time left on the window
I stare at the fragile reminder
Small, meaningless moments
      Life changing events
Masquerading as friends
      Disciplining as enemies
Spray on the Windex
An attempt to clear the smudge you left behind
Seems the print is between the two slides of glass
Can't wipe it away
Maybe I'll leave it there
It is all that is left of so much more

Fingerprints can't be burned away
Neither can the memory of you

Patrick Thorp Photography

Fear the Thunder

On days like this the thunder sounds so loud
Its pulse vibrates as it crashes against the window
Drops of rain pounding
Freedom realized in their fall
Each   Drip
          Drip
                  Drip
Another scream of ecstasy.

The ground is so shiny and inviting.

"Give me your tired…"

No longer will you fear the thunder.

Growing Younger

She can sit and she can cry
Can question all the reasons why
She grew up once
But then grew down
Once she could swim
But now she drowns

She chokes within her coffee cup
Each morning when it wakes her up
Her throat is clogged by every bean
Babies should not consume caffeine

A kid can hope for many things
For turtle doves and golden rings
Wasted wishes
For toys she begged
When should have wished for joys instead

Can't fish up coins already thrown
Or relight wicks already blown

Shooting stars won't light the skies
Once they fall
They cannot rise

Though each day her body ages
Skills revert to early stages
For years she walked
But now she crawls
She can't stand up
When she just falls

Since paralyzed throughout the years
Her only skill is making tears

Her body ages
Mind grows young
And to weak limbs
All dreams succumb

Full-Filling – Erotic

Acquire me
For all to see
Fake mystery
Shocked to see
Their expressions
No
    Not me
I like them there
Feeling their stare
Imagining
      Fantasizing
           Religion-izing
They watch our dance
Stance by stance
Physical romance
Beyond expectations
Sexual relations
That I conduct
To you instruct
How I like to get fucked

So here is the lesson
Please pay attention
I do love sex
However unless
My mind you possess
With intellect
You won't impress
There's no interest
To me there's no less
Than random sex

Didn't end the way you planned?
Get used to it
We women always have to…..

Charles Williams Photography

Drowned Abyss

Tears do fall upon this skin
Their salt made up from pain within
Drip, drip, drip, from eyes who've seen
A lack of love and loss of dreams

Tears fall and grounds are soaked
Flooding has since been provoked

Fear of drowning has commenced
As certain death can now be sensed

Hysterical, a mind can't think
Can't save itself from destined sink
Grasping breaths becomes so hard
For torn up lungs a life has marred

Suffocation now seems fated
As hope dissolves in life awaited

Desired fate cannot exist
While drowning in hopeless abyss

Tears continue and seem endless
Others walk and leave one friendless
Forcing one to become their own ship
As no friend can resolve their tears drip

Though difficult in a world of sin
Ships sails must be built within

Concoction is survivals need
To float and in a sense be freed

Lust Cannot Be 'Cause

Cold skin can find another's hold
Their touch hath yet to feel so cold
The heart that's felt is strong by need
Yet weakens with lusts gentle knead

Fingers relax instinct's consent
It's quieted, as walls descend
Allowing in what should be fought
A virus that invades ones thoughts

Its bug deletes all warning messages
Chews and spits out alerting presages
A healthy brain now turned to mush
Dissolved within lusts sinful rush

****

Provider can't be seen as wrong
While servicing a need so strong
Though candidate came unendorsed
Desires lobbyists coerced

Man obtained seat by lottery
To service him now forced to be
With principles she came equipped
From on soap box her legs can't slip

"Always adheres to moral laws"
Therefore, lust **cannot** be 'cause
True or false it will be proved
Though silenced...
      Instinct approved

I've Been…

I've been devoured

Fed a hunger stronger then lust
Pulled into a storm of starvation
Nectar created within my truth
Provided all nutrition to the soul of another

I've been consumed

Each morsel eaten up by eyes
That shined like stars
Brightening as they inhaled
An aroma of inner beauty
Emitting from the pores
Of a thin porcelain exterior

I've been laid down

Under a tree in autumn
Leaves, colorful security blankets
Dropped upon me one-by-one
Warmed me with words of devotion
Uttered from the strength of oak
The source that shed them

I've Been

Didn't Mean to Hurt You

Didn't mean to hurt you
Only meant the best
Felt all of the emotions
Pure and honest love
Saw you as my future

Your name was sketched
In my planner
Like on a tree
In a heart shape
Our names
With the carving
Of
"FOREVER"

We were going to plant that tree
Someday in the backyard
Of the house we would share
No idea where
That was just geography though

Our kids were going to climb it
They would have had your dark skin
With my green eyes
We planned them too
I really envisioned our children
That too wasn't a lie

Maybe I didn't really know you
When I believed
You were my soul mate
I did believe it though

Then you made me feel small
Lessened me in my mind
As all have done prior

Again I felt the frustration
Begging someone to see me

My goodness
True intentions
Pleading for them
To see my love as real
Defending actions
Not intended as perceived

The same series of events
Have plagued my relationships
Therefore my life
Too many times

I realized then
That as not all men
Could possibly make me feel this way
It must be in the choices
That I made in partners

Years of soul-searching
I've learned my pattern
So that I may never again
Follow the wrong path

I didn't mean to hurt you

However

I never intended you to follow my pattern either

Hidden Truth

What is hidden behind eyes
Truth envisioned or disguised?

Feel a sense of depth desired
Trick of mind or wish admired?

Fall within the thought of "you"
I cannot rise, scared of real view

Can't decide, fear or instinct?
Possibly the two are linked

Past has shown deed equals pain
Live without, acquired bane

Was a time too long ago
Making love was just as so

Insecure now, fear of passion
Used for others satisfaction

Hide behind a wall erected
Graffitied and then neglected

Abstinence - morals explained
Truth, its fear of feeling shamed

So much lies behind the scenes
Ignored, stuck on what is seen

Decisions now in mind conflicted
Fears construed, instinct predicted?

Assume all to be shallow
Other's faults on them bestow

Bricks built high but must still see
Otherwise the perp now me

Patrick Thorp Photography

A New Woman - Erotic

Another try
Another guy
A different day
Another lay
Another roll in the hay
For what you say
Who knows
I can't show
I know what I said
I'm through
Luckily this ain't true
I promised you
I wouldn't do
That thing I do
To make them swoon
To make them scream
To give them wet dreams
Possess their soul
Surrender my hole
To their control
I'll play the role
Who should I be
A wicked student
A slut - not prudent
A maid with a duster
Will u be my hustler
Make me beg
Make me want
To be taken
Never forsaken
For you to awaken
From a deep sleep
Living in a trash heap
No man to jump
No leg to hump
The garbage pumped
I'm ready
Are you?

'Cause

The smile does fade, appears for you
Dissolves only within self-view

Solitude now seems the trend
There this grin's safe to descend

The noble cause that knows my route
Drunken, stupid, stumbling about

Blistered by a sun that burns
Falseness daily now is learned

Once fantasized of fire-flies
Sparkling truth in another's eyes

History in mind now learned
Mystery for; shall not yearn

To give until there's nothing left
And in return; remorse, regret

Each time laying all my weapons down
Heavy to carry, needed around

Preempted were the wars infested
One has to keep herself protected

Silence sought in world too loud
Bullets ricochet around

Each screams out an evil word
Thought ignored but always heard

Against their pain, no safety vest
As each embeds themselves in chest

True heart bleeds an endless song
Verses of goals held too long

Odes to visions proven false
Source of which, now at a loss

Sleeping now avoids the truth
Knowledge I am their abuse

The Endless Stroll

I used to live within the night
Day time seen then only as a necessary passageway

Each morning the sun's rays brought me back to reality
Led me again down the daily road to the bliss found within dreams

Sleep was a place in which strength wasn't always required
There I wasn't forced to hover
Within a desperate façade of independence

Along life's roads,
Love seemed to be constantly yanked from my too needy grip
Yet wrapped within my comforter
The emptiness wasn't so cold

With age the walls of my room move closer together
Claustrophobic now, and the harsh reality of loneliness suffocates
As truth in the actual obtainment of happiness faded
So has the ability to even dream of its realization

No longer can the night be seen as a daily destination
Life however, is still lived within a constant journey to a dream

Still Searching

Rain pours down

Each drop
Another heartbreak

Though soaked wet with disappointment
She desperately seeks shelter from the storm

Many homes
Various "soul-mates"
Too many pills
To aid in too many diagnosed labels

She remains wet
And she remains at search

Looking for a place
Promised to her as a child
In the fairytales she was read

She's not Cinderella
She's not Ariel
Not a fairytale princess at all

She's just a person
       A woman
              A little girl
Lost in the rain

Insignificant and alone

Though drenched
She continues to search
For what she may very well never find
Praying that the rain

Nor her salty tears
Have filtered through her skin
To her biggest asset
Her heart

Before she was beautiful
Before she was accomplished
Before she was confident

It was strong
And it was good

She wants to protect it

But that need is blurred
By the rushing winds of the storm

Yet somehow
She remains determined

No author will write her
A "Happily Ever After"
She has to write her own

Yet, somehow
After years of fighting the rain
    So often
        So feverishly
And with such little success

She feels illiterate

Insatiable – Erotic

Insatiable: incapable of being satisfied

Freak me baby
For the Game
Sack me
Touch Down
Make me tame?

Not gonna happen
I want more
Much more body
To explore

Grab you firmly
Tight strong legs
Arms with flavor
Abs for days

Make me sane?
Not today sir
More to do
Molest me
And I will you

Lick you softly
Tongue your neck

Firm your member
Its turn's next

Billy the Kid Studios

Mechanics of a Broken Heart

Mechanics of a broken heart
An engine that's been torn apart

A useless charcoaled empty wedge
With wires burning at their edge
Marks of a self performed ligation
An attempt to avoid loves impregnation

Though the juice is its feed
Through holes it does bleed
Pierced by the cruel
Misuse of its fuel

Oil covers the wings
Can't flap when love sings

Pulled at the roots, each time enchanted
Until it was realized; only self can replant it

A dream of youth still not realized
Doubts reassured, and then goals resized

Can't rev up an engine that's battered and worn
With too many patches applied and then torn

Ticker weakened and too ill
To allow another spill
Of love and all it lacks to enter
To once again allow a dismember

Of the organ that still does pump blood
With time reigniting a once fragrant bud

Before Ever and Forever

Before ever
And forever
I've imagined you
What it would be like
To possess you
Undress you
Confess to you
I'm obsessed with you
Your image now more
Than an etching
In my dreams
Intensify feelings
Innately
Already strong
All I've ever known
Their strength now
Seems so unreal
Existing
For whom
I've never touched
But will
I love your voice
It soothes me
Each night
As I fall asleep
Secure
Just in words
Deep emotions
Adorn me
Detail my heart
Desires
That have always
Rushed
Through my veins
Scream louder now
All I hear

Is your name
Loud
Louder
Do you hear it?
My heart
Thump, thump
No matter
Where you are
My heart beats
In time with yours
Always has
Always will
Even
Before
We knew

Generic

Generic was your carefree stare
The noble morals that we shared
The way you touched me in the night
But just in dreams, out of your sight

Generic was the smell that stayed
Upon a heart that was betrayed
Believing a truth left unknown
A realness that was never shown

Generic was your too tight hold
As if I just fit in a mold
That was determined by the width
Of every woman you laid with

Generic was the way I felt
Each time within my soul you dwelt
Each time you pushed my kisses off
With words as cold as was your scoff

I've dreamed too long of just a dream
That never became what it seemed
Generic is this endless tear
That sheds for what was never here

Pale Skin Is Thicker

A look of awe within the eyes
That disappears when it's realized

A hunger found within a voice
That's shown in weakness, lost by choice

Can't fail to meet the standards set
If one forfeits with just pains threat

Umbrella blocks just scent of rain
Provides relief that is in vain
Its plastic shields the too pale skin
Ensures protection from rays of sin
Thickens with extent of enthrall
Nothing breaks through shielded wall
Its guarantee is for lifelong

"Skin stays light and heart stays strong"

Lonely is the ashen layer
That covers up an empty player

Partaking - Erotic

Erotic dream
Laser beam
Chocolate ice cream
Hot boiling steam
Fingers running down
Visiting my town
Roaming around
Maneuvering the crown
Awakening
Forsaking
Partaking
In the making
Self happy taking
Of what I know
My down below
Don't need to show
Myself the route
To turn one out
Without a doubt
I'll bring about
The end I seek
An extreme peak
Power technique
Satisfied
Redesigned
Unconfined
Freedom of mind
Body aligned
See you next time...

Big City Girl

Living in a tired world
Understanding just a curl
Lonely, sad "big city" girl
What a whirl…
      Never-ending
           Descending
                 Falling down
No more "big town"
Small town
Small
Me

Jaroslaw Photography

Sail Of Fate

Fate's dam opens and its waters flow
A storms rages and its winds blow

There is no control

My boat is forced from its falsely secure anchor
And it takes sail in search of its destiny

Life's a journey
I realize

But when will my tide come in
To take me to a land
Where the confusion of rough waters
Doesn't encrypt my mind

To torture me with an
Endless
Consistent
Unstoppable
Need to analyze all possibilities

Answers to questions I've possessed
Analyzed
And
Re-analyzed
My whole life

Through too many tragic storms
My bruised heart
The vessel on which I sail
Remains intact
In an ever quieting hum
It beats of hope

At sail I wait my turn
To reach a final dock

Where a truly secure anchor awaits

A home

Fate be more than just a hope
    Or waters
        I beg of you
            Me,
                Envelop

Rolf Bertram Photography

Once Lovers, Now Strangers

Summer turns to fall
Days become nights
Years pass by

And I think of you

Memories flood my unclosed mind
I can see your image in every corner
Hear your heartbeat in every sound
Feel your touch within each movement

Though your casing
Was intoxicating
Your shell
Was not your spell

Your outer image was blurred to my eyes
Clouded by the glow of your soul
Its light emitting from your pores

I followed the path of light
To your heart

To my death

Running
Walking
Crawling
Becoming
Paralyzed

My life passed before my eyes
As the memories do now

Torturous ecstasy
Certain death

At the edge of sanity
I "chose" to survive

Though promises of forever were made
They were not kept

Once the deepest of lovers
Now just incoherent strangers

Only in Deep Sleep Can This Be

Guilty by association
Presumed harms 'cause violation

Finally dreamed up the answer
Now she knows treatment for cancer

Alas her eyes find sight again
Within the rays this morning tans

Now back inside the space that's she
Space saturated with disease

She screams aloud just to be heard
Seems no one else can grasp the words

She fights each day to be released
Unshackled from the chain she be

To cringe with fear at every doubt
Too many doubts loiter about

Counts endless sheep, desiring rest
In sleeping pills she shall invest

She'll pass out to return to bliss
In bliss everything's happiness

Innocent till proven guilty
Only in deep sleep can this be

Merry-Go-Round

It isn't your fault I love you.
You've given me no reason to.

There was something in your glare.
Imagined.

A part-time lover when others lay you off.
With a switch you turn me on and off
Along with other females on your rotating platform.

Riding each in turn
You enjoy each gallop only within allowable measures.

An elusive mare stands out in a world of fillies.
Their trot less sure by step, my gait refined.
Exterior well groomed.
Red reigns shine and impress eyes.
Forced tinted lenses mute my obvious glow.

Neglected paint fades when it's not viewed in deserved awe.

My platinum pole's been scratched,
Carved to find an assumed wooden, hollow center.

Etched pits have remained patched with a reserve sign.

"Belongs to someone playing on the other side of the carousel."

My chains are now broken.
Roaming free.
Fleeing the pains of unrequited love.
Desiring to be seen as more than just another animal on all fours.

Me and You and Our Rendezvous – Erotic

Satin whispers
Thoughts prevail
Imagination wanders
When you're there

Answered fantasies
Sexy desire
Distinctive techniques
Light my fire

Skin on skin
Two become one
Engaging in combat
Until we're both done

Charles Williams Photography

Season's Riddle

Muscles ache to fill its void
Required to feel but pain
Fantasize of juicy nectar
Pulsating through veins

Each sample lesser then its prior
Never again to feel that high
Prayers seem to go unheard
Demand still greater then supply

Compliments are snorted in
Passion through injection
All men fall, swallowed whole
A diseased worlds infection

Frightened as the drug wears off
Street dealer can't be found
Lay amongst all desperate souls
Require one more round

Cupid's been incarcerated
Trafficking levels obscene

"Give them just a little bit
For life they now shall feign"

Rolf Bertram Photography

Torn Security

When my son was born I wrapped him up tightly in a blanket
The blanket went with him everywhere

He slept in that blanket between his mommy and daddy
Where a baby should sleep every night
The cloth was his security

I tore that blanket up piece by piece
Every time I left the house during the divorce

Tears of cotton and polyester
Tears of a level of consolation in the life of a child

His security forever disrupted

I've worked to repair that blanket
Hoping that a quilt will be more fitting
To a three year old boy

Still the tears are there and the stitches seem to be forever loose

No longer is he engulfed
In the warmth of the security he so deserves

Tonight he sleeps by me under a ragged quilt
Desperately longing for the comfort of his blanket

As I watch his little body
I can feel the fear within his dreams
And I pray with all that I have
That I didn't choose the quilt in vain

Jon Burdick Photography

My Biggest Secret

Pain forever
In just a few words

The sands of my future plans
Slipped from underneath me

I have two children

One I see and love every day
The other I have never held

I saw her once and I named her
A fetus only six months old

Chase Victoria

Her tiny hands waved inside me
I smiled as the Dr informed me
Of the medical prognosis
Too lost in her movements to listen

I knew she was a girl
Just how I knew Gavin was a boy
I just knew

She didn't force me to eat all kinds of sweets
Only a girl could be that understanding of vanity

We played games
Her and I
She kicked me
In the same spot I had just pushed at her

At night I held my belly so tightly
I thought I was protecting her

Seems I never had that ability

Everyday I continue on

Smiling and laughing
Crying and hurting

Yet, I never really continue on

How can you live
Without closure?

How can I ever move on?

When my child
    Never lived a day

Love in Lines

In noble dreams
There's no disguise

Your life for hers
You'd sacrifice

To be the king
Next to her throne

Dream to learn
Of the unknown

The lady that
You've waited for

Is now entering
Your door

You've dreamed of her
Through poetry

To hold her is
Pure ecstasy

The thrill you thought you'd never see

To touch her is pure victory

You talk of all the ways
You spoke

With hidden phrases
That you wrote

You hold her hand
And pull her close

She is the woman
You've loved the most

Restrained Dance

Over use and multiple injuries forced severe damage to her tendons

Graceful and elegant the ballerina dances on
Her abilities restrained from the pain

No longer can she leap as high as she's fallen too many times

Innately talented, she moves with skill and agility
Twists and turns inspire deep passion

Her private audience left mesmerized
Her performance awe inspiring

Always afraid of further injury she holds back
Restrains to show the extent of her talent and passion

Daily she finds herself fantasizing of the performances she will make
Her audience patiently awaiting her dance, allowing her to heal

Rather than finding contentedness in watching her move in pain

Playtime - Erotic

Will you be my toys?
Four in one to enjoy
My private playboy…

First as my rocking horse
I'll mount you with force
To prepare our eclipse
By thrusting my hips

Your wood will not soften
I'll ride on it often

Once you're prepared
With my hands you'll be shared
Back and forth they will fling
As I Yo-Yo your string

Pull up, down and steady
Trigger pulled and you're ready
To then toss one out
Of your water guns spout

Now to get me randy
Start licking my candy
Use all of your tricks
To get my girl slick
And then count the licks
It takes
To make
My whole body shake

A sweet lollipop
And the flavor don't stop

My mouth will then nestle
Your intricate vessel
And again you will float
As my wooden boat

When your sail is taut
Around it I'll wrought
And you'll ride the waves
While docked in my cave

A box I possess
For my special guest
If you'd like to stay

Come over…
                Let's play!

"She Writes Fantasies"

Stone Me

Stone me
Shun me
Cast me out
For the need
I must endow
The strength within
Requires green
Money
However
Is not that need

You Left Me Once

You left me once
I used to have to dream
To feel your arms around me

Now
When I awake
I see you

I walk through the forest of our love
Knowing very well
That at the end
Is just barren land

I wish to pause
        Forever

To feel your touch
        For eternity

But the wind of your kisses
Pushes me forth

So I go on

Not knowing for how long

Still hoping
That I'll never have to hunger
For your arms again

Why I've Been Late

Damaged in a perverse way
Goods delivered without pay

Heart for auction, state your bid
High or low, true value hid

Walls been built to avoid rough
Can't protect oneself enough

Defense stops only the mass
Few break through, it never lasts

Halls configured for just one
Others play his role for fun

Fearful of assumed belief
Incorrect and self-deceived

Deviant soon seen as false
Can't resume he must be lost

Thrown now from his secret whole
Eject man from seat he stole

Owner still to be made met
Soft entrance, not known by yet

Search continues, never ends
Excuse loneliness forced bends

Love for he, what threw me off
Wished too hard on just knockoff
Alarms stop their vulgar sound
Guards resume their normal rounds

Once again search for my mate
This explains why I've been late

To Obtain - Erotic

Enormous heights
I would obtain
To feel your touch
To moan your name
Uncover your secrets
Pleasure your soul
Roam your country
Rule your throne
Hear your breath
Taste your juice

See the shock
Of what I do
On your face
As it comes through

Your fingers
Press inside
Widen me
Prepare me
For what is to come

Will you play my strings?

Jaroslaw Photography

Vacant Hole

Memories fill this vacant hole
A lonely corridor
Once full of flowers
Tirelessly planted by your seed
Irrigated with your scent

Your aroma capsized me
Encapsulated my morals
I offered them to you within a gelatin case
Needing you to break inside

I begged you to enter
To consume each with a desperate force

The potent medication sedated you
And you lovingly slept within walls
That once stood painted with your artistic touch
Now left hopelessly naked of your graffiti

Sometimes
When I close my eyes
I blindly search the barren hallways
Of a space once illuminated with your scent
Now dark
Void of your passionate color

Pleasure is felt
But only as faint
As the memories
That fill this vacant hole

Graphic By Zelle

To The General Male Population I

So tired of the **desperate** ways
You strive to get yourself laid
It makes me sick how you will say
Anything not to delay
The orgasm that you desire
Me just the current flame of fire
Used to force your ego higher

I don't believe the shit you spew
A smart girl - I've figured out you
No - that is not plural
You're all the same
Full of shame
Different name
Different face
Became my own mace
Spray you off
With the cold fumes
Diminishing you
You will not me
For I am all I need to be

Helen of Troy
But I launch the ships
With the strut in my hips
The poutiness in my lips
My sexiness whips
Causes "men" to trip
Diving in for a kiss
They will miss
Few will prevail
To inside me sail

Claimed "adult male"?
Verbalizing with my pen
Once, twice and once again
"You are **Far** less then"

Don't need a boy toy
Ahem...
To be a boy's toy
How could I enjoy?
While you flex in the mirror
Stare at your exterior
Remark about your hot eyes
Measure your dick size
I have to enterprise
Got to get work done
Don't need another son
Not into going on an Oedipus run

You offer no education
Less then limited funds
Needing constant attention
Insecure not to mention
There's a new invention
It's called a job
You fucking slob

Like neon signs
I see your lines
They aren't new
No different view
No brain in you
Too dumb to date
Cannot orate
No thoughts to state
As you sedate yourself again
You are truly sad my friend

To The General Male Population II

Guess whose back
Yeah that's right
I'm the girl
Who likes to bite
Won't stop now
I'll give you more
Of all that sass
You guys adore

So, you're wondering
What's my issue today
Now what's this bitch
Got to say

Don't you worry
I'll fill you in
Perform aloud
Your ways of sin
So you love them clothes we wear
The sexy way we style our hair
Hot ass, long legs
Damn, those heels
Yeah, we girls got
That sex appeal

Drives all you men crazy
Your mind gets all hazy
"Isn't she a daisy"

Reel her in
Tell her she's "fine"
Then you'll get
That ass in line
Heels too high
Skirts too short

Too risqué
Such a flirt

You're the judge
We're on trial
Possible victim
One ego -
Witness hostile

You chose the hottie
Not the girl next door
But you can change her
Make her into what you've never longed for

'Cause when we meet
You love to say
How every man
Looks your girl's way
She is the one
You will not stray

Love the sex
Damn its good
Yeah
This girl has got your body understood

Want her, need her
Must commit
To the Lady
You befit

Once you have her
That'll change
It's biology
A guy NEEDS strange

Smile and No One Else Shall Know

Smiling decal, lips be sealed
Featured now and shall appeal
Always can appease a crowd
Acting tall and looking proud
Classy and elite she seems
Sleeping to retract the dream
People turn and people stare
Don't realize it isn't there

Whatever they are seeking
This woman isn't keeping

Shadow of a soul once was
Her figment deserving of applause
A ghost cannot be made a man
No matter how it's been planned
Cannot resume a life again
Diluted ink of pain in pen
Bitterness cannot recede
Love that's scared, cannot be freed
Favorite girl died long ago
Once meaning of life was known
Seen too much of ugliness
To find the beauty she does miss
Captured in a broken shell
Seeking to resume her spell
It's too late to reconnect
Gone forever, now forget
Live a life with half a soul
Smile and no one else shall know

Automatic Teller Machine – Erotic

Yours to create...

Offer statement of mission
Personal teller position
Provide now transcription
Of assumed job description

To give and receive spills
        Liquid, though not in bills...

Sequence of buttons pressed
Define desired request
Provide pin by desire
Wish and you shall acquire

No interest dismissed
        It is why I exist...

Key code now entered
Mid-body; face centered
My tongue now your mentor
Instructed by motion
I seek out your potion
Funds received in the juices
That my mouth produces

Routine to esteem
        Must be a machine...

Deposits been made
Next stage, now prepaid
Positions now switched
Your turn to enrich

Withdrawal buttons pressed
Laid out, you molest
Insert your card
Long, thick and hard

Keep pressing my button
    Without, she don't function...

Slow, fast, pace now steady
Sweet, rough and then ready
To disperse a portion
Of your saved up fortune

Wages spent in salary
    With a lifetime guarantee...

Continued education planned
Lessons to be learned firsthand
Degree sought from your college
Just provide me with knowledge

Teach me how and I'll be
    Your complete fantasy...

The Life of a Flower

Spring's sunshine and
April's showers
Reach to buried seeds within the ground

And they grow
Blossom to become more beautiful
       Colorful
              Sweeter smelling
With each passing day

Within its element
Its petals dance
      Its leaves smile
           Its stem glows
As it blows
In the breeze

When summer approaches
The flower cries from the heat
The tears soak its already welted petals
Dehydrate its already thirsty stem

The flower strains for water
Desperately fighting for life
It screams for food

Needing love once again
From the land it was created

But the love is gone

The flower fades
And slowly, painfully
It dries out

"I danced
I sang
I blossomed
I fought
Yet
No one will remember me"

And with that one last helpless thought

The flower curls up
And its life comes to an end

Its last thought
The only truth of it that remains

My Last Emotion

I forget how much it hurts each time you leave
Though I smile as you wave goodbye

So strange

But in this blurry world in which I live I feel almost nothing
I'm always driving too fast

This, I don't want to feel
Maybe if I drive faster...

But the pain is what keeps me here
It's the only emotion that I still fully associate with
The one I never want to lose
It is my last remaining connection to the world

It is my connection to you

My Prince
      My Savior

I sometimes yearn for time to sleep on the day daddy picks you up

I always forget how steep the pain is
And that each time you leave
I can't sleep
I just lay in bed with an overwhelming feeling of sadness and guilt

Sharing a child is like sharing your heart
It only beats blood through you half of the time

Jaroslaw Photography

While Left Dying

My funeral was today
Besides my friends agony and defeat
I am alone with endless tears
Left to die the same way I have lived

Buried six feet underground
The dirt covers my naked soul
Although I scream for air
My true desire is suffocation

The mud fills my needy lungs
Eyes blinded by the ever increasing darkness
No longer do they seek to search
As darkness is all they've ever found

I wish I'd had the money to purchase the wooden box
An extra the *Diener* had informed me
"Though short, your stay will be much more comfortable"
Comfort is something I've learned I don't deserve

The hours are passed with life's memories
Short term happiness always ending with long term pain
As the air within my new home dissipates
I remember the nothingness I leave behind

Diener - Gr., mortuary worker

Touch Unspoken

Knight of dreams, now just in such
Daylight kills the real of touch

Body naked, even clothed
Skin uncovered, left for froze

Starve for heart and can't possess
Hunger can't be quenched by rest

Hypnotized in stare of truth…
Not administered as viewed

Promises seen just in sleep
To myself secret to keep

Baptized by a touch ached for
Cannot fight in forfeit war

Promise felt by hands, unspoken
Still
At night
Desires woken

For his touch, a life been waited
Since been felt, need never faded

Can't rid mind of what consumes
His scent within each thought looms

Close my eyes, he's there again
Until sun-up sad heart can mend

Rays then blind what can't be seen
Visions from a mind deceived

Your Man - Erotic

You had him once while we were together
Seduced him with your whips and your leather

His mind forgot depths of true pleasure
Was a woman
Not a girl to mentor

Capable of taming any desire
Classy to be set afire

Legs that to enter
Oh…..
To get towards that center

With a mind in cahoots
A mental pursuit
Forgotten en route

Now he remembers
The joy in his member
When a beauty of such fine aware
Sucks him off beyond compare

A woman that could call his bluff
While always fucking him just hard enough
Will out do your lame
"Lay down and go" game

I think I forgot to mention…

Your man called me last night
He said that you can't work it right
Your shit just ain't that tight
Don't like to give him head
Words of passion left unsaid

Closes his eyes
 and sees me instead

While Beauty Fades

Take an arm or pierce the skin
No pain compares to that within
Depression is a life of hell
That sets a mind under its spell

Consumes all hope, the frequent thief
Steals the joy and leaves just grief
No defense can halt its hand
Against its plague no self withstands

Never can predict its arrival
Makes one wish against survival
All that's left is to wait it out
Ignoring all the guilt and doubt

Evilness controls the ride
Curl up until the pain subsides
Lay motionless while being swallowed
While sense of self slowly is hollowed

Another minute, another day

Just wait,
        While beauty fades away...

Too Good to Be Forgotten

When I close my eyes
I can remember your touch
The strength gained in your stare
The feelings of immunity obtained
From the heat of your breath upon my back as I slept

The confidence enveloped
Within just the sound of your voice

These memories encase me
Maroon me on an island
Where I am a princess
And you Sir
Are my Knight

Shielding me
From the pains of life

Self acceptance
Bred from your acceptance in me

Alas
There is no island
Lancelot is dead
Chivalry
Is just a dream

Confidence must be self born
No one else can save me

And with that understanding
I close my eyes
And remember what never existed

The memory too urgent
      Too necessary
           Too desired

To ever be forgotten

You

You come to me in the night
Whisk me away to magical pleasures I've never felt before

You hold me
Arms become vines
Entangle me in my hopes of forever

In your stare my fears and loneliness disappear
In my dreams your eyes hold promises
Invisible in the daylight

So I sleep to see your face in the beauty I remember

Your soul captured me in a cage
The key within my reach
I choose to remain imprisoned in torture
The pain; the only proof you existed in my life

Time
Look what's become of me…

The Ticket - Erotic

Queen of the Freak
Here now to speak
To talk the dirty
You all love in me
I give it raw
Stand it up tall
Drive you insane
Using only my brain
Imagine what I'd do
To the man I pursue
Never ending ejaculating
I'm good with my hands
My mouth follows suit
Electrically charged
Moving with pursuit
I'm granting admittance
My body your canvas
Do with it as wished
Hands pursuing
Pausing then resuming
Heat now extreme
Ticket redeemed
Enter me slowly
Inside then withdrawal
Erotically raw
Fill me with passion
Freely, un-rationed
Spill out your truth
Along with your juice
Enlighten more than "she"
Deal closed
You've got me

Any questions?

It Couldn't Have Not Mattered

They say "it's in his kiss"...

Were mine false?

I'm not the girl I used to be,
I know my worth

There are too many options...
What girl could be more than me?
I suppose many,
If my true beauty could be paled

I never was random;
It is always in my kiss
How could that have been missed?

There is still no thought more erotic
Then the expression on your face
Before our first and only real kiss

It couldn't have not mattered

The Apple's Sound

Apples fall upon the ground
Seemingly, without a sound
Their knowledge lost to many an ear
When fear was offered the wheel to steer

Those that lack a belief in fate
Will never reach its promised state
The road less taken is too long
It's only taken by the strong

If love is not found at first sight
For truth of it, all will must fight
Must fall in love with dream of true
And see the past within rear-view

The fight is hard, but true love resides
When belief in fate controls the ride
It's path is to the tree of truth
Where apples fall, and ears have proof

Billy the Kid Studios

Looking For Mr. Goodbar - Erotic

Twinkle, twinkle little star
Why must your vice be candy bars
Incessantly you seek your fix
Of Snickers, Almond Joys and Twix

Your tummy rumbles right above
A mouth that's hungry for a Dove
The two of you converse in heat
Turned on by every tasty treat

Left starving now for just a piece
A chunk of yummy stress release
Your voices seem to scream too loud
And from my pen they're spoken proud

"Shower me in dark with force
Mixed with softened milk
Of course
Fill my cherry with your cream
Make my ice cold lady steam"

A severe dilemma you cause me
Instant needs vs. moral's plea
A need to give in and indulge
In all the chocolate bars I bulge

Tonight I'll shut you up again
Play with you and your girlfriend
Tomorrow you shall only speak
Of Butterfingers path towards peak

Incarcerated

It suffocates and won't come loose
This endlessly reminding noose
Around a neck that strains for air
Yet somehow can't assume it's there

Oxygen in breath seems hidden
Within a life that pain is ridden

Chairs are offered with intent
To just delay and circumvent
Each time their pulled from underneath
It tugs and tightens on ropes wreath

Screams for help cannot be heard
No matter how loud the words
A world possessed by selfish needs
Cares little for this morbid plea

A room in which hope once sang
Is where this lifeless soul will hang

S & M

Chalk it up to insanity

Chained to your bed
A bounded masochist
Desiring domination

I am mentally branded
Owned
And controlled

My sadist
Now just a memory

Inflicted to a degree
That's criminal
The mental anguish
Remains

A warrant has been issued
For your arrest

The APB names you
AKA
My fantasy

Memories whip
And lust blindfolds

Bruised and tortured
The scars still remain from our last encounter

My heart a victim of Stockholm syndrome
Desires more pain

Cut me with words
Whip me with anger
Slice me to the core

"Abuse me"
Should be taped onto my back
Like a "Kick Me" sign

I belong to you
Do me
With me
As you'd like

The Survival of the Fittest

Stranded in the ends of time
A mind that needs to unwind
Living too much within a past
That pain consumed, and it still lasts

A view that still sees purity
Though only shown pure cruelty

Each and every person met
Is loved and proven a regret
They hurt a sore and beaten heart
While smiling as it's torn apart

All shreds of hope and fantasy
Are sliced for crimes, though not guilty

There is an image to pursue
Beauty viewed by any view
Beauty though has disappeared
Wept out and fallen with each tear

Assumptions made while viewing cover
Assumes there's no more to discover

Forced each time by will inside
To try to force a truth denied
The goodness is seen, but then ignored
Beauty does not come with such reward

Others survive by turning bitter
While true of heart shall only wither

Though always just misunderstood
When saw the world as full of good
The sweetened mind can't realize
A truth that offers its demise

Life would end with such resolve
So to bitterness, truth can't evolve

Combustible – Erotic

Set to Hot

Filthy visions
Evade this mind
Desires infiltrate
Set to unwind

Feelings of madness
Feigning for man
Needing the passion
Feeling the damn

Set to explosion

Fire within
Dangerous levels
Proceed with caution

Combustible
Fully adjustable
Giving style charitable
Sex need considerable
Gifted, like professional

Yours to corrupt
To screw and to fuck
Infest and to phase
Enter and amaze
Now set to ablaze

Dilate it wide
Enter the inside
Be still
Let me ride

Years of recalls
For shower stalls

Over and over again…

It's cold
Got a blanket???

Desired Apple

A sense of famine surrounds
Hungry suitors lure in their prey
Possessing a shiny exterior
The Red Delicious apple is desired
Lustful eyes starve and demand possession
The juice required to feed empty egos
Consumption means fullness

"Manufactured to Perfection"

Printed largely on the apple's seal
Wooers desire to rip the peel off
Not to read its contents

The apple too starves to be consumed
Awaiting the one who will pursue its core
Its juice slowly being squeezed dry
Sampled by manipulators who played the role
Each leaving permanent bites of falseness

Jaroslaw Photography

Spoil Me Baby - Erotic

Spoil me baby
Just tonight
Put on the music
Dim the light
Kiss me softly
Hold my hand
Pull me closer to my land
Exercise me
Tone my zones
Hydrate me
Be my hose
Penetrate me
Feel inside
Then sit back and enjoy the ride

Patrick Thorp Photography

Billy the Kid Studios

The Good Girl

A faded memory of truth
Reminder sensed from within youth

A girl once lived dies out with age
Through inner voice she speaks her sage

Trained to only show as good
Good heart rare, misunderstood

Right to reveal true self to thee
Dissolved each day since puberty

Tried to forget belief once known
A wall of fate too many stoned

Awake, then sleep, awake again
Days that pass; one starts, one ends

Another shall complete this eve
Passed same as last, in misery

If goodness only could be drowned
And evil, heartless soul be found

She'd carve out all the girl's remains
Empty her views to avoid pain

Though covered in too many sheets
Good heart glows, too loud it beats

It beckons all the needy souls
A fool she is and they all know

There's hunger in each corner passed
With her as feed, they shall not fast

If life was lived without the good
Though selfishly, she'd smile if could

Through The Window

The same window and the same view
Diluted by a heart once true
The grass was brown but viewed as green
The sky was black though blue was seen

The rain poured down each sunny day
Though skin felt wet hopes eyes betrayed
The world is not what once believed
Happiness shown was never retrieved

   Close the shades and return to sleep
   Shut down a mind that thinks too deep
   The scenes the same in dark or light
   Believed as good in black or sight

Sometimes ones faith can dissipate
A solid turned to gaseous state
Hope was dissolved within clogged air
Too many fates existing there

A cloud of smoke survives within
By bitter gasp it's taken in
Coughs can't relieve the empty pain
That saw the sun within just rain

   Windows deceived a heart of hope
   With sincere view mind couldn't cope
   Ignored what's true as light of day
   Painted sunlight where there's just gray

Window open, window closed
Eyes awake or eyes disposed
Ones hands can't shut the vacant view
And lonely eyes now see what's true

The world is full of black and gray
Pain grows in strength each passing day
Eyes hold new view, a different scene
Windows the same, but truth is seen

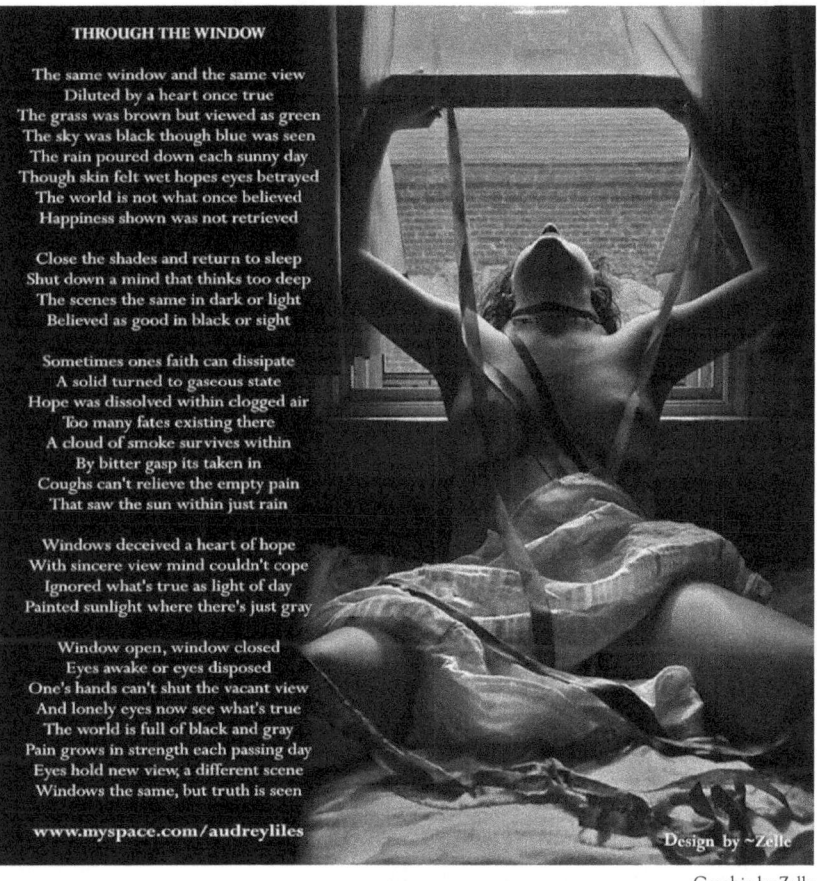

Graphic by Zelle

Passive

The sharpness of the cut glass end
The slice it brings could prove my friend
Death beckons me with welcome signs
Shines light inside a morbid life
Self–hate dissolved a dream of youth
Along with age came desperate truth
Tears rest upon this pillows edge
Urge on and on to jump the ledge
Escape a life of wretched pain
Along with blood pulsates through veins
A mold continuously tried to fit
Perfect in size, fit not a bit
A voice compels an empty hope
To fight, rage on or at least cope
Body is too weak it seems
To overcome brains fantasy
The beauty of a truthful smile
Lost inside a mind too wild
Thoughts eradicate this fruitful dream
To dissolve this nothingness it seems
Sleep and awake to feel such pain
Survival means to prove insane
Agony known, never new
A life of it as only view
Accustomed to a dark filled world
No longer with the light it swirls
Screaming for desired end
To drown the hate of unfound friends
Less of a whole to spread around
Good heart by evil self been drowned
Morbid thoughts that do not sate
Wish to force my death, my fate

While They Lay Sleeping

You can stare into the eyes of certain death forever
Daydream that within your glare the light to life can be found
No matter how intense the gaze displayed
Hope cannot burn through the chemical shield of an ailing soul

Poisonous are the meals consumed along the path to suicide
Each a sedation to the realization that only death lies ahead
Truth can touch a heart that bleeds ingested toxins
Though it falls upon skin too numb to allow its belief

Continuously kiss the forehead of a blacked out mind
Dream loves potion can somehow become the juice
That roams their veins, to suppress the hopelessness
And tame the raging seas of venom that resides within

Believe the word forever when it slips through lips
Too medicated to comprehend its meaning
As their possible endeavor towards forever
Is too short a passage to ever fulfill its definition

No grasp can hold the hand of a tortured mind tight enough
To vanquish the hunger for their truest adoration
Inhaled sin holds a beauty to which no human love can compare
As years blur into one never ending day of vacant survival

Recite a final parting prayer
Close your eyes and end your stare
To try to force a sight of light
Is to live within their darkness

Attention Deficit Hyperactivity Disorder

Sinfully absent
From my state of mind
Watching in past tense
The delay of the time

Driving in circles
Within my own head
Dizzy and nauseous
In a constant tread

Feelings of madness
Genuine, strong
Dropping by later?
I'll still be gone

'Cause inside my head
There is no one at home
Went out and got lost
Desperate and alone

Views always faded
Thoughts are astir
Wish I really knew me
But life's just a blur

Cupid's Broken Arrow

Cupid's arrow seems to be broken
Its aim is off on who it is poking

He promised that loves truth was ahead
Took out his weapon and aimed at my head

I closed my eyes and giggled in glee
Finally love was to happen to me

Directions must have been misread
It seems my dog was shot instead!

Once she was pierced, her loyalties shifted
Now onto the partner that cupid pre-gifted

She used to run around with mutts
Now with my man that bitch struts

My baby's been shot and he cannot see
His partner's a dog
It's supposed to be me!

Today he walked her down my street
Her tail in the air, she walked with conceit

I screamed out the window
As the two walked below

> *"She's not what she seems,*
> *She's just a missed bow!*
> *I waited a lifetime for you to pursue*
> *She'll never love you the way that I do"*

There was no catching my sweetheart's ear
Obsessed with my pet since shot by loves spear

Though cupid's intentions did come from his heart
He forgot to pre-test his component part

Love's truth was promised and did lie ahead
But my cage is empty and so is my bed

Sink or Swim

Flowers that live within life's sea
Grow towards the light of destiny
A sun that nourishes its days
With all the needs its roots convey
Sun's rays shine a light to fate
It burns all day

Until it's late

Sleep then offers
A dark nightmare
A dream that life's
Fate is despair
Words promised by just view of eyes
A night of sleep can prove as lies

Fear of that evil
Can leave a print
That remains past morning lights first hint
Smudges the brightness of a day
With fear, with doubt and disarray

A strength so strong
If forms a cloud
A cloud that bring showers about
Evil words poor down with rain
Liquid knowledge to the brain
It's hard for flowers to strain for life
If no good will come from all their strife

For a stem to grow
And for it to bloom
It must learn to swim
Through night's fear of doom

At Your Disposal – Erotic

At your disposal
Tempted beyond
Unending desire
Feel more
Touch more
Maneuver me
Pretzel me
Handle me
Torture me
Have me
Own me
Train me
Make me feel alive
Like only you can

Sketch By Jim McGee

Path Unhidden

I want to enter futures gate
To cut the metal around fate
Unleash myself from static rope
And run the fields of wished for hope

I feel the warmth that roams inside
Upon its back I yearn to ride
To fly above each endless mile
And feel the spread of a true smile

Each night within my dreams I've planned
The facts that live upon fates land
Blueprints been drawn within my mind
Its route will lead and I shall find

An artist drew a map within
Informs me how to stray from sin
It navigates and offers directions
To avoid temptation's intersections

Within my heart I've always known
Through inner voice always been shown
Ignored
But now I hear the sound
'Cause instinct is fate before it is found

A Naked Face

A smile can tell a thousand lies

Its truth unrecognizable to its possessor
Within the reflection of a mirror
Hung upon so many walls
By too many broken nails

Every night seems darker than its prior
And each morning's sun rises later
Awakens to shine without interruption
Upon a sidewalk once littered with the shadow of existence

Too many stepped on cracks
And a face is left to age naked
Except for a smile etched by the cruellest of memories
As an everlasting reminder of a once newly purchased mirror

Where did last fall's leaves go?

Credits

Photography

Billy the Kid Studios
http://www.billythekidstudios.com
Oldsmar, Florida

Charles Williams Photography
Tampa, Florida
http://www.charleswilliamsdesign.com

Chris Photography
Chris Omeara
Tampa, Florida

DevilDog Studios
Dave Parker
Tampa, Florida

Jaroslaw Photography
Jaroslaw Pietka
Tampa / New Port Richey, Florida

Jon Burdick Photography
Tampa/Clearwater, Florida
http://www.jonburdickphotography.com

Julio Cesar Custom Photography
Miami, Florida
http://www.jccustomphotography.com

Great Images Photography
Phil Grierson
Tarpon Springs, FL

Rolf Bertram Photography
Holmes Beach, Florida
http://www.rolfbertram.com

Patrick Thorp Photography
www.modelmayhem.com/patrickthorp

Back Cover Head Shot

Julio Cesar Custom Photography
Miami, Florida
http://www.jccustomphotography.com

Graphic Artwork

Kylerado Banister
Colorado
http://www.myspace.com/kylerado

Zelle Ladoux
Florida
http://www.myspace.com/erogenouszone

Sketches of Audrey Michelle

James "Mack" McGee
North Carolina
http://www.myspace.com/mackmm

Front Cover Design and Photography

Rolf Bertram Photography
Holmes Beach, Florida
http://www.rolfbertram.com

Book and Cover Layout

April Jack, all 4 design
San Diego, California
www.all-4-design.com

Author's Biography

Lori Zimit
Gaithersburg, Maryland
Sister of the author

Editing

Art Noble
Jensen Beach, Florida
Author "The Sacred Female"
http://www.**myspace**.com/thesacredfemale

Stephen Masters
Baltimore, Maryland
Freelance Writer and Editor

www.ingramcontent.com/pod-product-compliance
Lightning Source LLC
Chambersburg PA
CBHW071716090426
42738CB00009B/1791